Once a Derby Winner...

The Story of Barbaro

Cathie Katz

Outskirts Press, Inc.
Denver, Colorado

Outskirts Press
http://www.outskirtspress.com

ISBN-10: 1-4327-0494-X
ISBN-13: 978-1-4327-0494-0

Outskirts Press and the "OP" logo are trademarks belonging to
Outskirts Press, Inc.

Printed in the United States of America

In memory of my grandfather,
Donald Alexander MacDougall

Buttercups. They were everywhere as Barbaro grazed in the wide fields of Fair Hill Farm in Elkton, Maryland. He loved to munch on them, roll in them, sniff them. And while he was nibbling away he dreamed. He knew he was of noble blood, and in those fields he no doubt decided he was king of all he surveyed. There he plotted out the scenes of his many triumphs on the racetrack. He was going to win all of his races. He would listen to whatever Michael Matz, his trainer, told him to do. If Michael wanted him to run two miles a day he'd try his best. But his trainer was a very fair man and would never think of doing any such thing. He had mapped out a path that would take Barbaro to the Kentucky Derby and maybe even the Triple Crown in a very safe and careful manner.

First, Barbaro would run at Delaware Park, going one mile on the turf. There, as a maiden colt he was confronted with others in the same situation as himself. They had never won a race before and for most this was their first try ever. Michael had faith in Barbaro because he had shown in his workouts that he had a lot of talent and loved to run. His breeding, too, was solid. His sire, Dynaformer, was a well established Kentucky stallion and his dam, La Ville Rouge, was by the good racehorse Carson City.

Barbaro was bred by Roy and Gretchen Jackson, who owned a farm in Pennsylvania and had been in the racing business for many years. They watched as Barbaro grew from foal to yearling to a strapping two-year-old and they began to realize how exceptional he was. Gretchen especially was excited. The colt was big, good-looking, and bursting with energy. She was going to look forward to his every race.

Barbaro proved Gretchen right by winning his first time out. Not only did he win, but he did it with ease. He led the others by 8 1/2 lengths. Michael was proud of him. He had learned his lessons well.

© Lydia A. Williams

A month later Barbaro ran again, this time in the Laurel Futurity. And the result was almost exactly the same. Barbaro claimed the lead in the race on the far turn and then drew away from the field. He won this time by 8 lengths.

Michael knew by now that he had a good horse on his hands, and the feeling around the barn was one of great anticipation. It is always a magical time in the stable when a horse has the potential to become a star. Michael's assistant, an ex-jockey named Peter Brette, exercised Barbaro in the mornings. He quickly came to love the colt and told anyone who would listen how special this horse was. A friend of Peter's who was visiting one day looked deeply into Barbaro's eyes and decided that the horse was more than just special. He said that Barbaro was an old soul, that he'd "been here before."

Barbaro's third race was on January 1, New Years Day, 2006. And it was his birthday. In fact, it is the birthday of all thoroughbreds, who have this one official birthday as a way of keeping easy track of how old they are, since they run many races according to age groups. Most Thoroughbreds are born early in the year, before May, so they are all pretty close in age. Barbaro's real birthday was April 29.

In the Tropical Park Derby at 1 1/8 miles on the turf, Barbaro experienced another easy victory. He won by 3 ¾ lengths, and this time he had a new jockey on his back. Edgar Prado, one of the best jockeys in the business, replaced Jose Caraballo. Caraballo had ridden Barbaro in his two previous races but the horse's connections knew that if Barbaro was going to rise to the top of the game he would need a jockey with the skills of someone like Prado.

The Jacksons and Michael decided that it was time to seriously consider Barbaro's Triple Crown aspirations. They decided on a campaign for him that would take him through two more races before the Kentucky Derby. They were convinced that Barbaro belonged on that path. Some people doubted that the horse would be as good running on the dirt as he had been on turf, but Michael Matz said he wasn't worried. After all, Barbaro worked all the time on dirt in the mornings and did just fine. Why wouldn't he do as well in an afternoon's race?

The first real Kentucky Derby prep race for Barbaro came on February 4. This was the Holy Bull Stakes at Gulfstream Park in Florida. In it, Barbaro would meet other colts who were on the Triple Crown trail. The day of the race the track was wet and sloppy from the rain. But Barbaro didn't care. To him it was just another racing surface, another new experience. He trailed closely behind the pacesetter Dr. Dechard most of the way until, on the far turn, he took over and cruised home, daring the rest of the field to try and catch him. Great Point got closest, coming in second to Barbaro by ¾ of a length. But, though the margin of victory for Barbaro was less than it had been in his other races, he wasn't struggling to stay ahead. It looked as if he would surge on again if the closing Great Point got nearer to him.

As the Kentucky Derby drew closer many of those around Barbaro began to feel more and more that he was a magical horse. He walked with a confidence that not every horse had. He was calm and professional and regal. Everyone commented on how intelligent he seemed. And he was handsome! His coat was a bright reddish bay which glowed brilliantly in the sun. He had a large star on his forehead and a generous slap of white off-center between his nostrils. These markings made him very easy to spot.

Michael had one more race planned for Barbaro before the Kentucky Derby. This would be the Florida Derby, run at Gulfstream Park at the same distance as the Holy Bull, 1 1/8 miles. When the gates opened Barbaro stayed close to the leaders as he liked to do and then moved up to the front on the far turn. But today there was a horse who was unwilling to surrender the lead to him. Sharp Humor, who had led all the way, ran with Barbaro as he came up beside him. For awhile it looked as if Barbaro would not get by him, but with every stride Barbaro began to gain. Finally, Barbaro was up beside Sharp Humor and then pulled away. He won by a ½ length. But again, as in the Holy Bull, it looked harder than it actually was for Barbaro. He had something left in him and seemed to almost be playing with his rivals.

Finally, the day of the Kentucky Derby arrived. On May 6, Roy and Gretchen dressed in their finest clothes along with the other proud owners and waited in their seats as down below their horse paraded to the starting gate. They were confident of his chances, but, of course, a little nervous. Anything can happen in a race. They just hoped Barbaro got a good chance to show how talented he really was. They hoped he and Edgar got a clean trip. The Kentucky Derby is always run with a large field. So many owners want their horses to be involved in this historic race that the absolute limit allowed, 20 horses, nearly always enter the starting gate. But with this many horses all vying to be the winner, the Derby can seem a little bit like a stampede at times and if a horse is unlucky he can get trapped behind others and lose all chance of winning.

The gates sprang open and Barbaro bobbled a bit. He got right back in stride, though, and bounded away with the others. Edgar held him back a little off a quick early pace. Barbaro didn't need to be right up there with the others, who were setting fractions that were too fast for the 1 1/4 race. Barbaro settled nicely into fourth and stayed there as the horses made their way around the first turn and into the backstretch. The roar of the crowd could be heard even to the far side of the track as the horses and jockeys made their way around the oval. But it was nothing compared to the noise as the horses swung around the far turn and began to run for home. Over 157,000 fans screamed in excitement as they watched Barbaro take over from the pacesetters Sinister Minister and Keyed Entry. They yelled even louder when it was apparent that Barbaro was going to win, and win by a lot. He was widening the distance between himself and the rest of the field until the final margin was 6 1/2 lengths. The last time a Kentucky Derby winner had won by this great a margin was in 1946, 60 years ago, when Assault won by eight lengths.

Barbaro was now being talked about as possibly one of the all-time greats. People were saying that it wasn't so much that he had won all six of his races, it was the way he had won them – on dirt and turf, short and long, on sloppy and dry tracks, easily and battling another horse in the stretch. Few horses were so versatile. He had a jubilant way of running and one got the feeling he thoroughly enjoyed himself on the track and that there was nothing he couldn't do.

In the two weeks between the Kentucky Derby and the Preakness Stakes Barbaro rested up at Fair Hill Farm. He enjoyed his time there, once again being able to relax in its calm and peaceful atmosphere. Mornings he went out with Peter Brette for his exercise, and the two were often seen galloping through the early morning mist with Michael keeping a watchful eye on his horse. And later, of course, there were some buttercups to enjoy as he stood in his pasture dreaming of his future exploits.

© Lydia A. Williams

Finally the day came for the Preakness Stakes. Once again there was talk of the possibility of having a Triple Crown winner this year. Over the last 10 years several horses had come close, but not one had been able to do it. The last had been the great Affirmed in 1978. It is a very hard thing to win the Triple Crown. First, there is the Kentucky Derby at 1 ¼ miles, a very long distance for these young horses. Then two weeks later the Preakness Stakes at 1 1/16 miles, and finally in another three weeks the Belmont Stakes at a long 1 ½ miles. It takes a very good, probably great horse to do it. But somehow, after Barbaro's 6 1/2 length win in the Kentucky Derby and the ease with which he had done it, many people were saying that if any horse could do it, it would be Barbaro.

Barbaro was very excited on Preakness day. He was bouncing up and down as he arrived at the saddling area in the infield of the great old racetrack in Pimlico, Maryland. As the saddle was put on his back he had trouble standing still. He was so anxious. Maybe he was remembering his last race, where he had had so much fun running around that track where no one could catch him. Let's do this again, he thought. I can't wait!

His exuberance continued as the horses were paraded to the gate. He trotted, and bowed his neck and was up on his toes. As he stood in the gate waiting to start he finally couldn't take it any more. He had to go. A noise he had been listening for, that clang of a bell that told him when to start, sounded in his head. He had been listening so hard for the sound that he imagined he heard it when something a few feet away from him gave off a similar noise. He sprang forward. The starting gate opened for him because when a horse pushes forward and touches the gate it opens so that he doesn't hurt himself banging into it. He was alone on the track in front of the gate. He seemed to know his mistake at once because he merely cantered out and let the outriders catch him almost immediately. No harm was done. He was taken back behind the gate and reloaded. Edgar made sure to keep a firm hand on him as he sat waiting for the real race to begin.

The gates opened. Barbaro came out with the rest of the field. In mid-pack, with horses on either side of him he was where he should be at the start of the race. He and Edgar were running well, and the roar of the crowd came soaring over them from the right as they passed by the grandstand, crossing from light into shadow. Then Barbaro felt his right rear leg weaken. It was strange. But he kept on going. In the wild a horse who has injured himself has to keep going, running to escape any predators who will attack him if he shows any sign of weakness. All he knew was that he wanted to outrun that disturbing feeling. Edgar sensed something was wrong instantly. He could feel the change in the horse's gait, the sudden weakness underneath him. He pulled back smoothly on the reins, trying not to yank too hard. He had to help Barbaro now. He had to steady him and keep him from doing anything that would further injure himself. He steered Barbaro to the outside of the racecourse, out of the way of the horses who, in another minute, would be coming down that same stretch.

Edgar finally got Barbaro stopped, and he dismounted. It was hard to hold the colt, who was circling and moving around in confusion. Michael and Peter were there, as were others, and some were petting Barbaro, holding onto him, trying to keep him calm. And Barbaro eventually did become calm. His usual good sense was showing itself now. He merely seemed annoyed with his bad leg. He raised it slowly and then flung it backwards several times, as if trying to rid himself of the pain.

The fans who could see what was going on began crying. They watched fearfully as he was loaded onto a horse ambulance. The image of that regal animal being driven away, his head visible through the window, his behavior already so accepting, was something that would forever stay in their minds. Many were afraid that that was the end of Barbaro. Sometimes when a horse's leg is as badly damaged as Barbaro's appeared to be, there is no other choice but to put the animal to sleep.

But Roy and Gretchen Jackson called their friend Dean Richardson, a veterinarian who worked at New Bolton Medical Center in Pennsylvania. He was told that they were sending Barbaro to him in a few hours and that he was going to have to perform surgery to see if he could repair the broken right hind leg. Roy and Gretchen were determined to do everything they could to help Barbaro through this.

It was a sight to see. As Barbaro was placed in a horse ambulance which took him to New Bolton 70 miles away, police cars drove alongside, lights flashing, guarding the vehicle and clearing a path for it. A helicopter flew overhead, and on overpasses along the way fans were already gathered with signs written on sheets saying, "We love you, Barbaro" and "Good Luck."

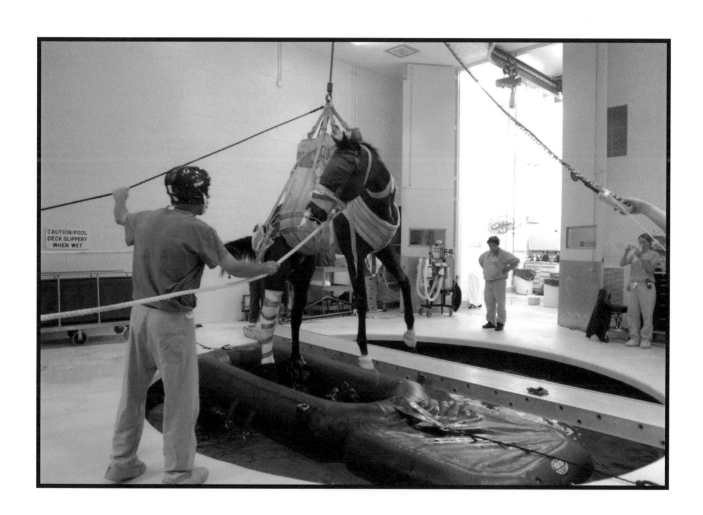

Barbaro's surgery began the following day. Dr. Richardson wanted to wait a day so that the horse could calm down from his ordeal and become more stabilized for the major surgery that was to come. When he did operate he found three bones broken, with one in multiple pieces. Dr. Richardson said he had seldom had to work on a horse with so bad a fracture.

After over seven hours of surgery, Barbaro was transferred to a pool which is used for the recovery of horses when they are waking up after anesthesia. Here they become conscious with their legs in the water while they float on a raft-like device. Then, when they are fully awake, if they begin thrashing around or become panicky they can't hurt themselves. But Barbaro barely needed it. He remained sensible and good natured throughout his recovery and when the time came to go back to his stall Dr. Richardson said he "almost trotted."

A long period of waiting was to begin for Barbaro and his fans. Barbaro became a model patient and won the hearts of everyone at the hospital. He was alert, always hungry, interested in everything around him, and sometimes frisky. Dr. Richardson was struck by his intelligence and charisma. A photographer who often came by to visit him and take pictures to record his progress noted how he seemed to know just how "cool" he was.

After those first few days life settled into a fairly routine pattern for everyone at New Bolton who was involved with Barbaro. They were now used to the daily deliveries of flowers, fruit baskets, carrots and cards that came for Barbaro. Signs appeared on the fences along the entry to the hospital, bearing various good wishes. Often they would simply say, "God Bless Barbaro," or "Believe in Barbaro." On June 10, the day of the Belmont Stakes, a huge seven foot high "get well card" was placed in the grandstand for the public to sign. Edgar Prado was the first to write on it. Another popular banner, showing a photograph of Barbaro's dominating Kentucky Derby victory, stated in a defiant manner, "Once a Derby Winner, Always a Derby Winner."

Dr. Richardson would visit his star patient every morning and Roy and Gretchen often brought him hand-picked grass. Michael and Edgar Prado visited as well. There began to be a glimmer of hope that perhaps Barbaro was actually going to make it.

Then, in July, Barbaro one day came down with the disease that Dr. Richardson feared would show up. Laminitis. It is a disease that strikes often in horses who are recoving from injuries to their legs because it attacks the good legs of a horse when he is trying to keep weight off the leg which is weak. Barbaro, as he stood in his stall day after day, would put extra weight on his left rear leg to keep the bad one safe. This extra weight damages the inside of the hoof and leads to the disease. There is often no recovery from laminitis. Dr. Richardson was fearful and tried to warn that Barbaro's chances were now very slim for recovery, but he made it clear that he would do everything he could as long as Barbaro looked bright and content and seemed to want to go on. And amazingly Barbaro looked just that way. He kept eating, he greeted everyone who visited him, and he appeared to be a happy horse.

So Barbaro's treatment continued. He stood in a sling many hours a day. Workers at the hospital were amazed by how he took care of himself. They said that sometimes when he was feeling pain he would stand next to his sling as if he were asking to be put in it. When he had had enough time in it he would fidget and ask to be taken out.

As summer came to an end Barbaro amazed everyone by continuing to improve. He was now taken outside to graze. Led by Dr. Richardson, he would spend a few minutes a day in the fresh air. He seemed to love being outside again and would gaze off in the distance as if deep in thought.

He had a good fall and early winter, and there was even talk of him leaving the hospital in the near future, but then in January new problems arose. His laminitic left hind foot was not healing as well as Dr. Richardson had hoped it would. In fact, it needed further surgery. Then, his now-healed broken leg felt the strain of trying to keep weight off the left leg. And finally, even though everything was done to keep up with all these problems, his front feet started hurting as well.

Dr. Richardson knew that he could do no more. Barbaro had gone through so much and tried so hard, but this was too much. All his legs now were hurting and to keep working on him would have been too painful for this brave horse. Roy and Gretchen and Dr. Richardson decided that the kindest thing to do would be to let Barbaro go. At 10:30 a.m. on January 29, they were all with the horse as he was given the anesthetic that would put him to sleep and stop his pain. He was patted and soothed and kissed as kind words were whispered to him. He closed his eyes.

Those who loved horses everywhere cried for him when they heard the news. They would miss him. He had become such a great and positive spirit in their lives. But his memory would live on. Barbaro had done so much good. People were saying that he had done far more good for racing than if he had won the Triple Crown. Because of his great struggle and bravery other horses would have a better chance to survive injuries in the future. New ways would be discovered in how to deal with laminitis and broken bones and the way horses reacted to slings, anesthesia and other medical procedures.

© Lydia A. Williams

And Gretchen, thinking back on Barbaro's eight months, was able to find one thing to be happy about. She was happy he was finally out of his stall. She thought about all the time he had spent there, quietly, contentedly, bravely, but still in a stall, when he should have been out running and prancing and kicking up his heels in the sun…the king in his pasture amongst the buttercups.

Photo Credits

Lydia A. Williams:
>Front Cover
>2
>4
>8
>18
>30
>32
>Back Cover

Vanessa Ng:
>6
>10
>12

Horsephotos:
>14
>16
>20
>22
>24
>26
>28